# DEDICATION

To my wife who makes this book and my life possible.
My children without whom I would feel empty.
Also to my parents who would let me drift away.

# Contents

# ACKNOWLEDGMENTS

To the people I have met throughout my life and to all I will meet. Thank you for what you have given or will give.

# How many times can we tell

How many times can we tell
They throw the penny into the well
Men push forward Women too
Just doing what they need to do

I will succeed says one man there
Do they see the others or do they care
They step over and on the people they pass
No care of colour creed or class

When all around falls down for them
They want to become your friend again
The attitude that they portray
Comes back to haunt them on this day

So when you make your million pounds
Just remember what comes around
If you step on me on your way up
My tolerance is not an empty cup.

# The eighties were the boom time years

The eighties were the boom time years
People partied with laughter and cheers
Now when we all look around
The party's over and they all feel down

I see the boxes in the streets
At the end are peoples' feet
Laying in the cold night air
Passers look they do not care

Its time for us to take a stand
And give us all a helping hand
Why should we all be made to eat
The bits left out in the bins on the street

Some people may just choose this life
To live amongst the trouble and strife

# We see the people in the street

We see the people in the street
Working just to make ends meets
They buy their food not always the best
After they've been on their little quest

9 to 5 is not for me
I only write when I can see
Not all of us can chug along
Hour and hour on and on

We all see problems roundabout
Can we help them should we shout
Will anybody want to hear
When we chant rage and jeer

No they just take us and put us aside
Because they want us all to hide
Our noises make those people quake
Because their glass world would break

Can anybody join this shiny nub
To drink inside the gentlemen's club
They don't want you if you squirm
Unless you are their little worm

# After the budget

The budgets finished some things have gone up
When will they listen and stop taking from the cup
All of the people wear a frown
Just when will this economy turn around

Watch the people how they try
To make things work but then a sigh
We try to save for a rainy day
But with the heating bills it burns away

When will someone let them know
Push and push only so far we can go
Why don't we have a vote on the deal
Then we can tell them how we feel

To every person I would like to say
I doubt they will ever give us our day
To tell them what we really know
It's time to let us have a go

I wish I could write about good things
The flowers bloom and how birds sing
But all I see is doom and gloom
They say it's the recession after the boom

I wish I could remember the good old days
When every sun had a redden haze
But from my book I've lost that page
When working people had a good weeks wage.

# Window Watching

Staring from my window I see the passers by
The cars in the street the orange red sky
It's passed the noon and not quite eve
The darkened clouds they do deceive

You see the lights come on in haste
For night times here and time to rest
Have you been working for today
Or letting the hours just pass away

# Watching the world go by

Just sitting here watching the world go by
I'm getting the pictures in my mind's eye
The children playing the games of fun
Enjoying life everyone

Please look deeper then the surface cracks
The world is slowly dying on its back
We need to look at what we've got
Before it goes and we lose the lot

Why should we wait upon the end
Until so broken we cannot mend
The wreck that we leave is then passed on
To the people of tomorrow and on and on

# Work for life

People work for all their life
Hoping to cope with all the strife
I look around at what I see
It's not so good, is it only me

We hear of all the good time hence
It seems like chat over the garden fence
Many don't make their ends meet
They starve to put shoes on their kids' feet

It must be time for us to say
Give us all a fair days pay
The politicians keep the seeing blind
Look out for the elder of our kind

# When

When we the people see the plight
Of people sleeping by day and by night
Under paper under a bench
The rain comes down they all get drenched

The soup kitchens come to give for free
Blankets soup or a cup of tea
They take it but they feel despair
At least they know someone cares

Lets go back to 1710
Has time stood still or moved forward since then
The people still sleep rough and suffer
The only thing missing is the candle snuffer

Why don't the bigwigs look around
And see us sitting on the ground
Most of us did not choose
To sit around without our shoes

I ask you all to stop and look
In every corner cranny and nook
Don't just tut and say what to do
Because one day it might be you

# Broken Down

I'm waiting for that awful sound
I'm sorry but it's broken down
Do I mean the television or car
No. It's the country we see afar

The only thing I have to say
Its already happened before today
None of them will turn and state
The horse has bolted now shut the gate

I look upon our island here
And think it's time for us to care
Why can't the people turn and note
If we were a vessel we would not float

What problems? We can hear them say
I don't need to worry because I'm okay
Why should they sit and listen to us
We're the lower class who makes a fuss

Give us figures then string us a line
And tell us that everything is fine
I think it's time to listen to me
I'm not so blind I cannot see

We need to look at the older face
Deep in those lines we can see grace
Pride in the country that once stood
All working for the common good

# That's it I quit

Sitting around looking, watching the world
Hoping everything will work out
Watching all the children working hard at school
Learning, that's what it's all about

What do we want to follow us, a race without a clue
Or do we need a generation who can pull us through
I've looked at what they're doing, it leaves me very cold
These kids we see are our future, when we get old

Let's make the learning system enjoyable and fun
Get the teachers working hard to help everyone
I don't know how we've done it but it's all just slipped
People need to look in the pot not just in the lid

# Growing

During our life we all grow up
Experience fills our empty cup
The road of life is never straight
The good things not served on a plate

Which government do we choose
To control our life and to abuse
They take us first into our schools
And furnish us a set of rules.

They teach us how to do our sums
And help us all with what is to come
Then you move to your next school
And then your given a new set of rules

This next step in your life is new
But you'll get taught just what to do
You learn your science bit by bit
Throwing, running, jumping in a pit.

Now it's time for teenage years
This part will only lead to tears
You study hard to make the grade
After this you'll wish you stayed

Now it's time for you to leave
Through the world and to the grave
When you look back did the system serve
The education you deserved

# Rushing

I'm sitting on this speeding train
The tracks run through the earth like veins
Industry speeds across this land
Taking bits with every hand

I think it's time to put things back
Try to shorten the growing track
Look out for every person free
Education is the key

Get the people who are on top
To take a stand and put a stop
To the waste of our people's life
To remove all of the trouble and strife

If we start at the end
We end up going round the bend
The children are the human race
Very soon they'll take our place

Let's all pull to show them right
Give them a more informed foresight
Teach them all what's right to do
This will help both me and you.

# Help Them

I look at the things around the world
The old the young and infirm
We don't seem to take much care of them
When will we ever learn

I think it's time to step outside
This world we live in now
And make this place a better place
For all of us somehow

# When

When will it happen
When will it change
When will the route be rearranged
When will the people sort out this way
When will we wake up to this day

# Education

I think it's time to put pen to page
I'm sorry I'm not a wise old sage
What are we doing to our young
Voting on their education

The government should find the cash
And sort out all of this terrible mash
Build the schools, get the staff
To create the country that will last

Look after the seed the roots grow strong
The stem will lift up on and on
The bud then opens and will flower
Then with colour it shows it's power.

# Building

I've looked at people again and again
Seeing what's around
After careful thought
I'll tell you what I've found

Pyramids are built from bottom and top
But this is where my comparison stops
For a reason that's unknown to me
We seem to start at the top of the tree

I look at the face of an innocent child
The passion for life drives them wild
But we insist, this we should stem
And make them toe the line again

We seem to say let's get things right
And let the elder study by night
Get the adults working well
Give them jobs that's what we tell

Why don't we take a page from a book
Settle down and have a look
If we build from bottom to top
Who knows where this success will stop

If we can educate the children well
Where will it end who can tell
Will we become just what we were
A nation when we were proud of her

# Looking

Sitting in the sun I leave my mind.
I look across the space what can I find.
Half of the people are content.
The rest feel like their time is spent.

Maybe we should start again
And then should try to find
The way in which we can be
Help for all mankind.

Our younger generations
Have to go without
The things that should be free for them
To that there is no doubt

The elder of the human race
Are treated with disdain
We should learn all they have
We won't see that again

# Who is it

This is just a very short line
To tell you everything is fine
That's just the thing you need to hear
To give everybody a good cheer

An answer to the question you ask
Who should we just take to task
The politicians have a splintered behind
To say they sit on the fence is kind

# Hidden

As Monday follows Sunday
Of that there is no doubt
But now it's time for people
To get up and give a shout

Look at what we're doing
All around our land
It's time for us to shout out loud
Get up and take a stand

Let the people know just what we really feel
Why should we be treated like a dog and then be brought to heel
As soon as one man makes a stand we see just what to say
Just as he is noticed he's politely put away

# A look at our island

From the tip of John O'Groats to the bottom of Land's End
All the people on our isle, their money they do spend
We all need to earn our cash to give us self-respect
But the jobs are not around to help us all to connect

Look at all the figures they are just like films
Fiction, Fiction every one reels and reels and reels
Two Million, Three Million, Four Million now
We should have another look at the crowd

I think it may be time to tell us all of us the facts
The work of ages has gone and will not be coming back
Maybe we should look again to see what we can do
To put the people back to work or school for me and you

# Discussions

I listen to the radio many people call
The range of opinions differ men, women one and all
This is how it should be, us all to have our say
Why should all the governments tell us, ours is the only way

I believe it's time to think again for the people in their tower
And maybe let us share a slice of the controlling power
Look at what the parties say we haven't got the money
If they were a public limited company it would not be very funny

The monies gone the countries shot we all just need a hand
To deal with all the problems but not just in our land
Please look around the world at these problems we have got
Let's all sit round the table and stop this stinking rot.

# Dreaming

I have thought to look around to what is the state
Of all the people sitting round with an empty plate
Some people here are heard to say remember the good old days
Murder, war and robbery oh what wonderful ways

Now why have I just thought of this when my life should be fun
Because the mist of yester-year has got me on the run
All the people should wake up and see what's just around
Now live to make the world a place where fairness can be found.

# What's Missing

This country was built on it's industries
These things they all seem lost
What is the island going to do
They worry about the cost

Where is the pride we all once had
The things that made this country glad
To be able to stand up straight and proud
And not hide under a darkened cloud

# To Ponder

Let's all sit here and put the world to rights
Stop the famine, wars and fights
It has to be done before this country will be
Part of the European community

We can tell them what we need
It's our vote that should make them heed
The nation put these people in
We can take them out again

You are alarmed to voice and say
On how you want the world today
Don't be beaten on your brow
This is your world, you should say how

I look around our capital town
At this time I wear a frown
It's 6 am the people sleep
In the doorways on the streets

Now kids can't get what they all need
The knowledge to life the learning seed
Then look above the system provided
Our horizons are widened and guided

We go out to do our work
Our responsibilities not to shirk
But then we hear your pay's the same
Its not up this year again.

Now it's time to hear us shout
This style of government should be out
The people who are the elected system
Don't have the common sense within them

They look down on us but say
The people here are all okay
I think it's  time they all awoke
Before our country is completely broke

Let's go back where I began
Stop us becoming an also ran
Make the people here proud to say
England is where I want to stay.

# Sharon

I've trudged around the streets again looking for a job
My feet are sore from walking to earn a couple of bob
Now I've been told you are too old or your experience is just too much
I cannot give you an easy job your qualifications are such

I start to feel I'm going down life's great big plug
But I can't let this happen so my shoulders start to shrug
This puts a strain upon me because I'm normally so high
The one who looks upon the troubles and spits into their eye

I bend down to tie my shoe laces to pull them with a  tug
Maybe what I really need is for you to give me a hug
I understand I sometimes confuse you with my words
I do not mean to do this and sometimes I'm absurd

For you, if I could I would change the world and make it all alright
But sometimes you don't understand I do get full of fright
I do believe our luck will change maybe not overnight
But I can only work with it and try to make it right

I wish you would just talk to me when something causes pain
Cause when you don't I get the feeling I'm going down the drain
I understand you talking to anyone you want
I'd never stop you doing that, point of fact I can't

Maybe I don't listen and I know I should
Because all the things that need doing, together I know we could
Let's look upon the things we've got and the things we've done
We're blessed with a  wonderful daughter and three wonderful sons

I'm sorry if I shout at  you, it might seem that I don't care
I love you more than anything on that fact I swear
Let's not lose sight of what we've got and what we can achieve
Together we can beat the world and see what we receive

I know you sometimes get fed up with the things I do
But things would never be the same if I could not be with you
I want to take you in my arms and say things will be alright
I need to know you will always be there for me every night

I'm sorry I can't get a job I will keep looking round
I'll also try my best not to let things get me down
Sometimes I do say things to defend just me
But I know that you have every right to expect better things you see

Sometimes we do get told things that do wind us up
And we should ignore those people and tell them to shut up
I am guilty of this, but sometimes so are you
But I don't mind you telling me because I'm always here for you

I wish I knew the answer to every little thing
I don't, but I do try to find them and do it with a zing
At the end what I am trying to say is something I should do
With all my heart I want to say Sharon I LOVE YOU.

# Why

Why do we all just turn the page
Why is it we are full of rage
Why are people running lost
Why does it call come down to cost

Why should we all sit and wait
Why should we have an empty plate
Why are the answers not around
Why can't the remedies be found

# In A Rush

I'm sitting on the morning bus
Watching people make a fuss
Trying to get to their work
Responsibilities not to shirk

Some of them look so full of strain
In their faces you see the pain
They take a seat if they can
To show there not an also ran

Working on the days agenda
Pricing up the new work tender
Watch the energy they use
Let's hope they don't blow a fuse

The end of the day the work is done
They see the bus they start to run
On they get and pay the fair
Tidy the workload, comb their hair

Now they've come to the house
To spend time sitting with their spouse
Have the dinner, watch the telly
Have a bath when their ready

As they sleep their mind it turns
Their body for the daylight yearns
To get back to the daily grind
To just sleep settled would be kind

xxx

# The Children

My children bring me lots of fun
From the rise to the setting of the sun
The life within them is so abound
Just watch them play and run around

When does this begin to stop
People say it's time to grow up
Why make them do this at such a pace
They are all part of the human race

Let them spend as much time as it takes
Have their parents eat their cakes
Don't force upon them all the hurry
Don't give them all our adult worry.

# Drifting

I look upon the midnight air
The gentle wind blows through my hair
I come inside, into the room
Knowing the morning comes too soon

Night then joins up into day
My weeks just seem to slip away
Sometimes I wish I could see the light
The end of the tunnel should burn bright

Then a thought comes into play
Pull yourself together today
Get up with a brand new smile
See what happens for a while

# Thinking

I think it's time to take a thought
What we do is what we're taught
We can all make up our own mind
Explanations we can find

At the start we go to school
Learning, learning all the rules
Then we hope we get a job
Earn for us a daily bob

With this money we can obtain
A life that's full, save a bit for rain
But at this time the thought it stops
Our pockets are full of empty drops

Our umbrella becomes our house
We sit quiet as a mouse
The public are fed hours of telly
About as good Ice Cream with no jelly

There are people who don't have a bean
They can remember what they've seen
Its long ago, food they bought
It may be time to rethink this thought

# We Wait

Let's have a look at the overall view
The people standing in a queue
Signing their name every week or two
This could be me it could be you

People tend not to understand
Why we queue or why we stand
Because we don't have a job
It doesn't make us slobs

Have you ever looked around
Thought and put ideas on paper down
An idea to solve our problems here
How to make our lives sincere

# Not hearing

I listen today at what we're doing
Putting children out to work
Should we listen to our elders
Or to the occupants of our schools

We hear the children are not listening
To the teachers telling the facts
Is it that we are not teaching
Us just talking puts up their backs

A person of the age of fourteen
Should not be called a little kid
They are young adults if you look
Now listen to their bid

Now what we need is assistance
From them and from us
Can they get us all to listen?
NO! All we do is curse and cuss.

# Share It

I'm Looking at the things around
No one smiling just a frown
Could this be the times we live?
I don't think so more should give

I'm not talking about their cash
The guilty conscience just to smash
Experience and expertise
These are the things the people need

# Invisible

Today I looked at parliament
The old men looking so content
They go home to their large abode
Passing people lying in the road

Spare some change they do not hear
The noise of snoring in their ears
Do they just walk with their eyes blind
The people of the streets they do not find

Is the outlook oh so bleak
Or is it just control they seek
They're the masters, we are the slaves
All worked until we're in our graves

The ministers say it's getting warmer
Recovery is just round the corner
The shoots are green taxes down
The monkey's going round and round

After sixteen years of having a go
Why do they need to make a show
We all know it's coming to an end
The welfare state, the nation's friend.

# 2010

I take a look fifteen years hence
No more sitting on the fence
Cameras, passes forced control
watching everywhere you go

If you've got no money no food to eat
Can't get clothes, no shoes for feet
Lets get the people to look around
Not only at us on the ground

If you've no money, you can't know
The education to make you grow
You will not learn how to read
Not even how to plant a seed

If you've no money, you will become
The underclass, everyone
If you're sick, you're shown the door
To the hospital for the poor

The one thing I can take from this
Is something has just gone amiss
Back to nineteen ninety five
Help the people to survive

# Teach Them

Now have I been a bit unfair?
Just looking at the world so bare?
Do you think my view is clouded?
Are my eyes appearing shrouded

All our children should go to school
learning things, not playing the fool
Can we see the education
For all the children of our nation

From humble beginnings we all come
to meet the dawning of our sun
We are the same at the start
Blood, mussels, bones, a beating heart

Some of us our paths mapped out
Captain of industry no doubt
But I think this should be noted
Education for the quoted

If your parents can stretch and reach
The money it takes for us to teach
You will learn about the Apollo rockets
If they put hands in their pockets

One of the things I want to see
Is education completely free
For all our children without exception
All highest standard no rejection

What I'm saying, is it so absurd
To teach each child the written word
To help them all to use their brain
To start the circle going round again

Maybe it seems, the things I say
Are obvious to us today
Then can you tell me why it's not done
For every daughter and every son?

# Discover

Looking in the paper, I see so many jobs
I liked to stay within my field to earn a couple of bob
No No No you must retrain
To start your career once again

Now all the unemployed can see
This retrain scheme does not mean
A job for which you are ready
Not even employment that is steady

Let's all try to sit and think
And find the answer to
The problems we all face today
Not just me and you.

# Dreaming

It's now 3am, the people are asleep
Listen to the noise and see pictures that they keep
Inside their head incumbent in their dreams
Hope, successes, happy life, not always as it seems

I wish I could make the journey into these people's heads
Helping all their wishes come while lying in their beds
Could someone help all of us to make our dreams come true
To help the wants of everyone and not just me and you.

# Fixing The Thought

Take a look around
See the people on the ground
Some with a smile upon their face
But most just feel they've fallen from grace

You hear them discuss their cares and woes
Are these the answers, who knows?
They try to solve the world out right
But nothing changes by the end of the night

Should we all get round the table
And solve the problems when we're able
Take from them the permanent frown
Try and stop them from being down.

## ABOUT THE AUTHOR

I wrote these in 1995. When I look back at them now, how they still apply has made me publish them.
**The Sound Of An Insignificant Voice** ©.

CPSIA information can be obtained at www.ICGtesting.com
Printed in the USA
BVOW031102130612

292553BV00001B/89/P

9 781469 912653